PUSSIFUR
and the
SEARCH FOR HOME

A True Nantucket Story

Thomas M. Fletcher

New Moon Press
Newton, Massachusetts

ISBN: 1460998693
ISBN-13: 9781460998694

Printed in the United States of America
Set in Book Antiqua

Contact the author by email at tomfletcher@rcn.com

www.nantucketpussifur.com

To Janice

"Once upon a time" is how many fairy tales begin. This story happened once upon a time, too, except that it is a completely true story from Nantucket Island. It really happened. What is so good about true stories is that they can show us how close we can get to hard times and still try for a happy ending. This story is like the winding, windy course taken by sailboats in Nantucket's Rainbow Fleet. It has lots of twists and turns and choices to make—with an ending that might surprise you.

Our story begins in the big city of Brooklyn, New York, where a happy, friendly family with four kids lived in a nice, comfortable house. The house was not big. It was a simple one, made of red bricks. It had a colorful, green front door and a couple of front steps that the kids could sit on in good weather. Their street had lots of these pleasant houses built side by side. Each house had a small backyard and a front yard that only took a minute or two to mow. The four kids who lived there had plenty to make them happy—including the main character of our story, their cat named Pussifur.

Pussifur was a pretty big cat. He had a gray tabby coat with black, tiger stripes on his gray fur. He had patches of snowy white fur on his neck, face, and legs. Pussifur could be a playful cat, but he was also patient, calm, and very smart. He had been the family's pet cat for nine years, so all the kids had grown up loving him.

To a cat, Brooklyn streets had lots of activity and lots of people. There were many kids who picked you up. It seemed like every kid had a bicycle that went very fast on the sidewalks. And, because there were many houses on the street, it meant there were lots of big speedy cars. Pussifur knew he had to be very careful on his Brooklyn street because everything moved so fast there—except in the cold winter.

When there was a big snowfall on Pussifur's street, nothing moved at all. To people it might have looked pretty, but it was not a fun time for cats. On those cold days, Pussifur would just sit inside the warm house and sleep between mealtimes. In the winter, he was mostly waiting and dreaming—waiting for the summertime and dreaming of his most favorite place.

What Pussifur loved most about life with his family was what happened in June of every year. Once school ended, the kids would pack suitcases and bags with their favorite things for their summer trip. Into the bags would go shorts, T-shirts, and sandals. Bathing suits, beach towels, and water toys. For rainy days, the kids would pack games, playing cards, crayons, and story books. When the packing started, Pussifur would climb into a suitcase, too. He figured if he did that, maybe the summer trip would start sooner.

After everything was packed, Pussifur's family would load it all into their car. What couldn't fit inside their long white station wagon would get piled into a huge bundle on top of the car. The first part of the trip would be a drive of many hours, so the cat would mostly sleep. Since Pussifur couldn't read, he didn't really know how to get to where they were going, but he knew that toward the end of the long drive there was a big bridge. When the car got to that tall bridge, the kids would call out, "We're here! Cape Cod!" That would wake up Pussifur, and he would begin to get excited.

Soon the family would arrive at a dock where a big ferryboat would carry them and their car to where they were going—the faraway island of Nantucket.

The ride on the ferryboat was not much fun for Pussifur. The people got to jump out of the car and go up to the top deck of the ferry where they could be in the sun and watch for Brant Point lighthouse as the ferry entered Nantucket harbor.

Pussifur had to stay in the closed-up car down below, missing the fun. Big long trucks would get parked right next to his car on the dark ferry. These big trucks were important because they carried everything that Nantucket Island people needed. But they were very noisy and a little scary to him. And the ferryboat's loud engines that pushed the ferry through the water were right next to his car and the trucks. It was hard for a cat to curl up and sleep. Pussifur looked forward to getting off that boat.

Pussifur knew that the long drive from Brooklyn and the noisy, sometimes rough ride on the ferryboat were all worth it. He knew when they were getting close to Nantucket because his family would all come back to the car. When the long boat ride to Nantucket was over, driving down the ramp onto Steamboat Wharf in Nantucket was wonderful. The kids would roll down the car's windows and Pussifur would feel the island breezes in his face. It was one of his favorite moments of every year. It meant summer finally had arrived!

Summers on Nantucket were the absolute happiest of times. Pussifur and his family lived outside of town in Polpis at a place that had once been a farm. Over the years, the house and barn had been fixed up a lot. The main farm house was old, but cozy. It had a bright, white fence around the courtyard and Nantucket Blue shutters that matched the clear blue summer sky. Flowers grew in the old well and in window boxes.

People still called Pussifur's place a farm because it had wide open spaces for running in at full speed, and giant maple trees for climbing high over the rooftops. An old chicken coop and a barn were getting fixed up inside so that people could live in them. There was bright, warm summer sun to lie in, and the cool sea breezes kept the air from getting too hot. Over the years, many wonderful old things about the farm had stayed the same, but some things had changed.

Instead of the chickens and sheep that had once been raised on
Pussifur's farm, the animals that lived there now were the kinds
that lived in the bogs and bushes and moors all around Pussifur's
huge yard. These animals were perfect as Pussifur's playmates. He
could chase the bunny rabbits, and play hide and seek with the
garden snakes, and even try to catch a bird once in a while. No one
had to worry about speeding cars or bicycles.

Life on Nantucket couldn't get much better, Pussifur thought. While he was having fun chasing wild animals and climbing shady trees, his family was doing people things. After their morning chores were done, the people would mostly go to the beaches and ponds to play in the sand and waves. Almost every day included a "squantum"—the old Nantucket name for a picnic. Sometimes the squantums were under the big shady maple trees that Pussifur would climb. Other times, they would be at the beach so that the family could stay by the water all afternoon.

The night time on Pussifur's Nantucket farm was mysterious and fun. It was a perfect place for a cat to be roaming in the dark, waiting for the rabbits to come out and play. It was also the favorite place for neighbor kids to come after supper and play flashlight-tag in the big yard. In the moonlight and under the stars, kids would hide in the bushes and in trees and around the corners of the houses, waiting for the best time to run to home base without being seen. It was hard to imagine days and nights with more good times.

The only part of every summer that Pussifur didn't like was when he could tell the family was getting ready to leave Nantucket. They would talk about doing things "for the last time"—picking wild blueberries for the last time, or going to Sankaty lighthouse for the last time, or walking around 'Sconset for the last time. He never liked leaving the island. So in his mind he would make up a postcard of those "last time" island scenes.

One summer, after another playful and restful time on Nantucket, Pussifur noticed that the family was starting to talk about leaving. But something was different that year. He decided to hang around in the house and figure things out. He stretched out on the floor and closed his eyes, but kept his ears on alert while his family talked.

Sure enough, it turned out that the family was planning a very big change—a move to the other side of the world, to a place called Singapore! The problem was that it was too far away to take all their things, and especially they couldn't take Pussifur. The family talked about what to do with him. If they found him a new home in Brooklyn that would end his visits to Nantucket, and they thought Pussifur deserved something better. Pussifur's family would have to work hard to find him a new home where he would be happy and safe. No one was sure whether things would work out well for him.

Pussifur definitely agreed that if he were going to have to give up his family, his wish would be to stay on Nantucket Island. Maybe he could live outside at the farm on his own? He had heard that the cool fall weather turned the green grass and green bushes into pretty yellows and browns. The bunnies liked the fall, but he worried about outdoor life after the fall became the Nantucket winter. It got very cold there, with howling, freezing winds. No wonder his family left after the warm summers. If alone at the farm was not a good idea, where was he going to end up?

Pussifur's family was worried about him, too. They first thought of walking along the dirt road to ask neighbors if they could give him a new home. But almost all of them left Nantucket for the winter and others already had pets.

When finding a new home near their farm didn't work out, Pussifur's family put an ad in the Nantucket newspaper asking for anyone who could give their cat a new home. But no one called; no one reading the *Inquirer and Mirror* was able to help. Finding Pussifur a new home on Nantucket was not working out very well. Pussifur deserved something better than this.

Next, the family visited the ferryboat of-fice. The people who worked at Steamboat Wharf were always friendly, and they lived on Nantucket all year long. Maybe they could help? They said they would be happy to make Pussifur a wharf cat and let him eat the fish scraps left by the local fishermen. When Pussifur heard this, he thought it might be fun to spend the day watching the fishing boats in Nantucket Harbor. The salty air and ocean breezes would smell wonderful if he lived by the wharf. For a cat, eating fresh fish at every meal would be a dream come true!

But the ferryboat people and the fishermen would not be able to take care of him all the time. It might get lonely and a little scary when the sky turned wintry gray. He would get cold, wet, and hungry on the wharf with no one around and no home to go to. It looked as if finding a new place for Pussifur on Nantucket was not working out.

Pussifur deserved something better than this.

The end of summer was getting closer and Pussifur still didn't have a new Nantucket home. One of his family's last ideas was to call the animal shelter. They always had pets there for people to adopt. The nice people there said they could take another cat, but only for a little while. They would try to get someone who lived on Nantucket to adopt a grown cat like Pussifur. The problem was that kittens were more popular, so they couldn't promise that things would work out happily for Pussifur. His family agreed that Pussifur deserved something better than this.

Cats don't usually worry about things, but even Pussifur was getting a little worried. He knew there was little time left in the summer. Soon the harbor would be empty of summer boats and the bright summer blues would start turning winter gray. His family would be moving away soon and no one knew where Pussifur would be living. His family knew they had to keep trying to find him a new home. They couldn't lose faith in Pussifur's future. Where would they go for their next idea?

Every Nantucket summer, St. Paul's Church on Fair Street in town holds a popular street fair outside the church. Hundreds of people come for the all-day activities. There are clowns and games with prizes. Cooks and bakers sell delicious food and treats to eat. Artists and photographers sell pictures of the island. Colorful handmade crafts are sold. All the money earned helps the church's programs for the needy. And, this particular year, Pussifur's family added a new attraction.

In the middle of all the noisy fun of the street fair, one special table was set up. On it sat a nervous and worried Pussifur in a basket with a sign that read "Free cat to a good home." The large wicker basket was decorated with a bow to make it look like a present for someone.

All day long, Pussifur's family told people his story. But all day long, the friendly people would just wish Pussifur good luck and say they couldn't give him a new home. The family was hoping for someone, anyone who would help Pussifur. His family was running out of time and ideas. Pussifur deserved something better than this.

Then, as the afternoon sun began to move lower in the sky and many fair-goers left town to go to the beaches, a small woman wearing a flowery dress and a broad-brimmed straw hat came walking by Pussifur's table. She was carrying a large white bag and a red box of chocolate-fudge treats. Walking with her was a woman who was helping by carrying two heavy, full bags.

The woman in the hat slowed her walk as she passed by and read the sign on Pussifur's table: "Free cat to a good home." She stopped, thought for a few seconds, and asked pleasantly, "What is the cat's name?"

"Pussifur—because he is such a furry cat. He is a very friendly, playful cat, too."

"I must say, he is also a very big cat," the woman remarked. "Does he ever get into trouble or mischief like some kittens and cats do?"

"No. He is already nine years old and behaves very well."

The pleasant woman reached into the cat's basket and scratched Pussifur under the chin. Pussifur tilted his head for more scratches, and started to purr with happiness that someone was showing an interest in him. The woman smiled at Pussifur and stepped back from the table, turning toward her helper.

No one at the table could hear what the two women were saying to each other. Everyone in Pussifur's family had fingers crossed, hoping that this was the good news they had been working for. Finally, the pleasant woman in the hat turned back to the table.

"I'll tell you what I'll do," she said as she wrote something down on a slip of paper from her purse. "Since we have our hands full with bags, we can't take the cat right now. On this paper I am writing my address in town. In about an hour or so, bring the cat with all his things to my house." She nodded toward her helper. "You can leave the cat with Hermie, my cook and housekeeper. If the cat doesn't jump up on the kitchen counters or claw the furniture, we'll consider keeping him. Is that agreeable?"

Pussifur's family was very grateful to the pleasant woman in the hat. They thanked her over and over, promising to bring Pussifur to her house at the end of the afternoon. As the two women walked away down the street, Pussifur's family quickly put him in the car and headed home to get the rest of his things. They wondered whether their cat would be happy with the woman. They knew nothing about her or what kind of house Pussifur would be living in. All they had was an address in town written on a slip of paper.

When Pussifur and his family got back to their farmhouse, everyone was having mixed feelings. They were mostly very happy that they had finally found a possible home for Pussifur. They also were a little sad that they might be saying good-bye to their cat.

While everyone was inside getting Pussifur's things packed, Pussifur went outside alone one last time. He sat by the courtyard fence and looked out across the yard at the former barn that was now a cottage. It was hard to imagine that this might be his last look at his summer playground. And, it might be the last day he would spend with his family.

Pussifur was given a scratch and a hug by each family member and put back into the car for another trip into town. He began to be excited about his new adventure. He was very curious about exploring a new place. Pussifur being mostly curious and excited, rather than sad, was not surprising. That's pretty much the way cats are.

The address on the pleasant woman's paper read "93 Main Street." Everyone was so busy getting Pussifur ready, no one thought about where the address was. The family figured they would drive to the beginning of Main Street where the stores were and then just follow the street and its numbers until they found "93 Main Street." So they were not prepared for the HUGE surprise that was in store.

It was a quick, five-mile drive down Polpis Road to town. They drove past the Shipwreck & Lifesaving Museum and past the fresh vegetable stand at Moors End Farm. Once through the rotary on the edge of town, they headed toward the wharves and the harbor. There they turned left onto the famous cobblestones of Main Street.

The car and Pussifur's cat basket started shaking as they drove over the bumpy cobblestones and up the slight hill past the three blocks of Main Street stores. Past Mitchell's Book Corner and Murray's Toggery Shop at the end of the Main Street shops, they continued along Main Street into the part of town where there were tree-lined streets with houses.

Pussifur's family started looking at the numbers on the Main Street houses—69, 73, 81, 85. They could tell that the woman's house would be on the right side of the street since 93 was an odd number. As they bumped along slowly on the uneven cobblestones, they began to realize something they had not stopped to think about since the street fair—all of the houses on this part of Main Street were big and old and elegant.

As they got closer to number 93, they stopped talking. The car pulled up to the curb and stopped. Everyone got out and stood next to the car, staring in amazement at the house and its number—93. Could this possibly be true? Someone took out the paper from the woman at the street fair just to make sure they hadn't made a mistake. It read "93 Main Street." There was no mistake.

The car was parked in front of 93 Main Street—one of the most famous houses in all of Nantucket! Because it was so famous, Pussifur's family already knew all about it. Many years ago, back in 1837, when Nantucket was known as "the Whaling Capital of the World," the richest whaling merchant in Nantucket was Joseph Starbuck. He owned several whaling ships. The beautiful brick mansion at 93 Main Street was one of the houses Joseph Starbuck built especially for his sons.

What made the brick mansion at 93 Main Street extra special and famous was that it was one of three matching houses. The very rich Joseph Starbuck built three identical brick homes next to each other for his three sons—George, Matthew, and William. Joseph Starbuck wanted the three matching houses to last forever, so he had them built of strong red brick. It was expensive and unusual to build brick houses on Nantucket, and because the big and beautiful houses were built side by side, they became famous and were known everywhere as "The Three Bricks." Today, you can walk or drive up the cobblestones of Nantucket's Main Street and see Joseph Starbuck's Three Bricks—East Brick, Middle Brick, and West Brick—still standing handsomely at 93, 95, and 97 Main Street.

Pussifur's family was amazed that the famous house at 93 Main Street was about to have special, personal meaning for them. "Pussifur," they said, holding him up with great excitement, "it looks like you might become the luckiest of all cats! You have the chance to live in Nantucket's fabulous East Brick. Whatever you do, make sure you behave yourself overnight so you get to stay here."

Hermie had seen Pussifur's family drive up and she came out to greet them. She stood on the top step, wiping her hands dry on her white apron and smiling at Pussifur. She said she was sorry she couldn't invite everyone inside. She explained that the pleasant woman in the hat, whom she called Mrs. Fonda, was not home and she, herself, was busy in the kitchen preparing dinner. But she thanked the family for bringing Pussifur and promised to take good care of him overnight.

The next day, as they had agreed, Pussifur's family telephoned East Brick. They were hoping to hear that Pussifur had not broken any house rules on his first night in the elegant mansion. Hermie, the friendly cook and housekeeper, answered the phone. She was happy to say that Pussifur seemed to be the perfect cat. She said that Mrs. Fonda, the woman in the hat, had been happy to have a cat around. The Fondas had just bought East Brick that year, and they all agreed that Pussifur would make a nice addition to the family. They also decided that Pussifur would keep his name. So it was all settled—Pussifur would stay as the new cat in Nantucket's famous East Brick!

Pussifur's second family lived happily for many years in East Brick. They made it one of the great homes of Nantucket—filled with beautiful antique furniture and a large library of rare books. Over the years, Pussifur became special to them. Mrs. Fonda was most happy to have a large, handsome cat who would charm all her house guests. She even had a local artist come to the house and paint a pastel portrait of her Pussifur. The portrait hung in the garden room where visitors would see it. And so it was, that years later, while on a tour of Nantucket's historic houses, Pussifur's first family would see the painting of Pussifur and know that he had been loved in his second Nantucket home.

Over the years, Pussifur's first family also felt that things had turned out well. Through hard work, their dream of living in a faraway country had been a good thing for every family member—even their cat. They knew that even though some would say that Pussifur was just a cat, they had shown their love for him by making sure he, too, had the best possible chance at happiness.

Pussifur's first family, after a couple of wonderful years in Singapore, moved back to a new city. And to this day, they return every summer to enjoy the quiet country life of Nantucket. Today, there are new family cats who, like Pussifur, enjoy chasing wild creatures around Pussifur's first Nantucket home— a place known as Squantum Farm.

As far as Pussifur was concerned, life had turned out perfectly. While he was a kitten and a young cat full of energy, his family had been one with playful children who enjoyed active summers visiting the Nantucket countryside. Later, when he had become an older, grown-up cat, he stayed in Nantucket year round, living the comfortable life of a pampered mansion cat with loving, quieter people to care for him. He became well known to many tourists and townspeople who would go by and take pictures of him—the big cat guarding the front steps of the famous East Brick.

So, I guess you can say that, as in any good fairy tale, everyone in this true Nantucket story of Pussifur the Cat lived happily ever after.

ACKNOWLEDGMENTS

When I first heard the story of Pussifur, I loved it for its perseverance and charming triumph. Special thanks to my wife, Janice K. Fletcher, and her mother, Gladys Keidel, for their accounts from the summer of 1969. Details that time distorted were corrected with the help of the fine folks at the Nantucket Registry of Deeds. Internet searches led me to Mrs. Lois Fonda. My thanks to Mrs. Fonda, her daughter Paisley Haller, her son, Jelles Fonda, and his wife, Kathy O'Connell, who after forty years verified details and completed the storyline. The latter two are keepers of the Pussifur pastel.

I received frequent on-island encouragement. Special thanks to Mary Jennings of Mitchell's Book Corner, Richard Duncan and Jean Grimmer of Mill Hill Press, and Elizabeth Oldham who was invaluable in editing and fact checking historical details. Don Fletcher, Marilyn Keith, and my immediate family were helpful critiquing my early manuscript.

The illustrations represented a new challenge and a cherished process. Special thanks to Ed Wilson for encouraging me to pursue artist software as a means to producing them. Elements from 137 photographs were used in creating the forty illustrations. Fourteen of those pictures were historical to the period. Three of the illustrations feature the real Pussifur. In addition to my images, source photographs were taken by Keith Keidel, Janice Fletcher, and Beverly Hall who provided the images from the St. Paul's Church fair. My thanks to Deanna McCormick of St. Paul's Church for securing the permission to use the church fair images.

Many family and friends appear in the illustrations, including cats: Katie, Prinkin, Macy, Folger, and Starbuck—our frequent stand-in for Pussifur because of his remarkable similarity in appearance. Special thanks to Yvette Ruffin who modeled for several illustrations.

Finally, I offer my love and gratitude to my wife Janice who supported and encouraged this book in every possible way.

8607064R0

Made in the USA
Charleston, SC
26 June 2011